The Top Reasons Why Relationships Fail

By

Benny Ferguson Jr.

ISBN:
978-1-7354117-8-1

Published by: The Ferguson Company

Editor & cover design:
http://roxanec.wix.com/time-to-read.com

Welcome

Relationships between human beings, instead of being a beautiful exchange between people, are now often a thorn, a source of pain and constant frustration. It is critical to realize that the beauty and purpose of relationships far exceed the brief emotional charge that they create. They can leave a lasting, lifelong imprint on all who are affected or influenced by them. It is your turn to recognize just what may be the failing marks of your relationship encounters. If you were to find them would you correct them? If you were to correct them, would you see significant results in your experiences? My answer is emphatically, "Yes". You are more than just a participant in a relationship, you are its maker, and the image that you sketch becomes your masterpiece. Take this work as a guide to uncover your shortcomings in relationships, and allow the guidance within to shape your relationships anew.

You Have Not Let Go Of The Past

Your past will destroy you if it consists of negative, virus-like symptoms, and you allow it to infect your present moment. Your past does not infect those you come in contact with, only you. Attempting to protect yourself from a past event re-occurring pretty much guarantees it. Whatever you put your focus and energy on grows. It grows mentally because you carry around the image of the past event. It grows emotionally because you continue to feel the past emotional effects it had on you. It grows behaviorally because you attempt to steer clear of the experience by behaving in ways that protect you from it.

Attempting to protect yourself from a negative experience does not align you with a positive one; it further separates you from it. The only way to create the relationships you desire is to let go of the past and focus on the present moment. You must focus all of your thoughts and emotions on being, with all your heart and behaviors, the type of person who experiences the relationships you want to have.

Cheating/Infidelity

The deepest commitment that is broken between two individuals can be an end or a beginning. For most, infidelity is the end of all, and symbolizes the dissolving of the relationship mentally or that there was never true commitment to the relationship from the beginning.

In a few cases, where understanding is gathered by both parties, it is discovered that cheating or infidelity was a cry for help, a longing for mental and emotional needs to be met; those that were not or could not be met by the partner prior to the occurrence of infidelity. In such cases the end of old patterns of behavior and the start of new awareness and understanding creates an even greater bond and level of commitment.

You must decide in which category you and your relationship reside.

Too Comfortable

Familiarity can be a blessing and a curse in disguise. In relationship, familiarity and being comfortable can yield less effort to connect and truly understand each other. It can give way to comments like, "My partner understands, or should understand."

Being comfortable also leads away from the effort put into being an awesome partner, the effort that was put in when the relationship was new. When you stop caring for, supporting, and being concerned for the well-being of your partner; when you stop choosing to be your highest self in the relationship, you become a person that your partner does not know. You become someone other than the person that your partner fell in love and wanted to be in relationship with in the first place.

If being comfortable is affecting you, address it directly. Communicate your needs and how you view the relationship at the moment. The responses you receive will give you insight into the best and most direct future courses of action.

Bad Habits

Your habits in the use of bad language or in the demonstration of reprehensible behavior can cause severe damage to your relationships. Physical abuse can readily been seen and the pain only lasts for a time. Mental and emotional abuse, however, goes on and on, and their effects can cripple a relationship and a person for years to come.

Be mindful of whether your words and your behaviors are building up or tearing down the relationship. If you are suffering from a partner's bad habits, communicate their effects to that partner directly, and use those responses as information when making future decisions.

Outside Interference

The entertaining of outside interference is the slow death of relationship. Unwarranted opinions, negative biases, skewed perceptions, and jealousy can all play a part in chiseling away at a healthy relationship.

Be aware of the information or guidance you receive from others. Is the source credible? Have they demonstrated success in their own relationships? Are they free of ulterior motives including attempts to protect you from being hurt by the relationship in the event it ends?

The highest level of communication is like the doctor of old recommending you to take a couple of aspirins and calling him in the morning. It is nearly the cure–all of most relationship ailments. Seek outside advice for how to make things better, on how you can be better or more in the relationship. Only communicate discomfort and struggle to those who will give you unbiased, nonjudgmental, solid advice. If you do not have anyone around you who can provide that sort of support and advice, all of your answers can be found in a book. Jump on the internet and scan tables of content, or head to the nearest public library.

Moving Too Fast/Pushing Too Hard

It is possible that you or your partner are not ready or may never be ready for certain levels of relationships. Pushing for the sexual engagement in a relationship can quickly create doubt and concern for a partner's true intentions. Also, pushing too hard for the idea of marriage can jar a relationship into a downward spiral if a partner is not or has not reached the same level of readiness.

Many connections have failed because 'good' sex in the beginning was mistaken for a 'good' relationship. Many marriages have failed because marriage in itself does not equal relationship, nor does it secure you from the inherent challenges that arise from two human beings living in close quarters.

Develop a strong relationship first. Get to know each other, the good, the bad, and the ugly. How well do you work together as a team? Pay attention to your partner's behaviors. This is the true-tell all of their inner thoughts, ideas, and level of commitment.

Good sex does not equal relationship, and marriage does not equal relationship. Only relationship equals relationship.

Different Priorities

Two individuals having differing ideas about life and the direction in which they want to go is not something new. Recognizing that this is the case for you and your partner only indicates that it is decision time. Can you work together in support of each other's goals and dreams, or does the chasm appear so great that there is no possible way to work together? Either decision shows your personal strength, but do not choose to let your goals and dreams go in support of another's by any means. The inner conflict between the life you live and the life you desire will potentially become a thorn in the relationship.

If you are aware, through strength of conversation, that you and your partner have priorities that are clearly poles' apart, but the relationship is there, it is possible that the team can still overcome and ultimately win together in the short and long term. If the relationship is not there, pushing to stay together will only create greater and recurring conflicts.

Dependence vs. Independence

There is nothing greater in a relationship than two strong individuals choosing to come together, to unite forces in the creation of life and love. True independence and strength supports its partner, encourages, and is not swayed by fear or insecurity. True independence loves unconditionally, and is not easily moved from that position.

Dependence is needy, fragmented, and looks to others, to its partner for validation and fulfillment. It is quick to blame and to attempt to control because its emotional coffers are often depleted, because they are not being filled from the inside. Dependence, in the end, becomes a burden to its partner, a drain, and creates so much stress on a relationship that it, and its partner, begin to suffocate bringing death to the relationship.

Yes, there is a natural complimenting that occurs when two individuals mesh and develop a relationship. However there is balance in the compliment. A partner who is dependent creates a huge imbalance in a relationship.

Discover who you are and what you require personally, mentally, and emotionally. What can and should you be to yourself?

When you are strong, whole, and independent, you will attract a partner who is strong, whole, and independent, and the complement between you two will be remarkable.

Age Difference

The difference in age between two partners does not have to be the determining factor in a relationship. Yes, there may be differences in experience. That is everybody. Yes, there may be differences in understanding. That is everybody.

The question is, can the individuals be treated and regarded with love and respect in spite of the varying levels of experience. As a team in a relationship, can an equal level of position and power be maintained in spite of the difference in age and experience?

The truth is that which appears to be the challenge posed by age exists even when a difference in age is not a factor. Also, any greater responsibility that may be assumed by the older partner may be assumed by the younger when age becomes a challenge for the partner on the upper end of the scale.

Age between two adults is only an issue if you allow it to be. If you are doing the correct things to attract a complementing partner, then age should not be a factor when that partner comes along.

Economic Status

The disparity in economic status between two partners is an issue of mindset. A partner that has never had to base their decisions on a possible lack of money is going to think and feel differently than an individual whose buying decisions have always been based on whether they can afford an item or not.

Because the idea and issue of money mistakenly carries so much emotional weight, it takes effort to overcome the binding that a lack of money can bring, but it can be done.

If you are a partner who has always had money, be sensitive to your partner's hesitation to spending. They may be the perfect balancing agent for you, but do not let their hesitation begin to block the flow of money that you currently experience. Your belief in money, its abundance and existence for and to you is a plus.

If you are a partner who has experienced and believed in the lack of money, and has never had a lot, recognize that not all people have experienced or believed the same as you did. Your partner may be your catalyst to higher and greater thinking and believing in the area of money. Recognize the barriers and insecurities that exist inside of you in relation to money, and quickly begin to let them go so that the flow of money that exists in your partner's life can also begin to exist in your life.

Gender Confusion

The role of two partners in a relationship, when it comes to the male and female role, is an outdated strategy. The new strategy when it comes to partners committed to being together is simply to work as a team. Are there chores that either partner likes to do and volunteers to do? Does one partner's income make it feasible for the other partner to remain home and take care of the business of home and the children?

These are simple questions to be entertained and decided upon by the team, for the greater good and workings of the whole.

Gender should not dictate the roles in a relationship. Likes, dislikes, and inner guidance as much as possible should be the guides, and you will find that a balance will emerge.

Again, if you are doing the right things inwardly to attract a complementing partner, roles will not be an issue.

Lack Of Sacrifice

Lack of sacrifice is an issue in a relationship when you go into the relationship feeling as though sacrifice is a necessity.

True relationship is based on trust, support, encouragement, recognition, understanding, and unconditional love. Under these circumstances, what sacrifices need to be made?

When you have a goal, you are supported and you support your partner. When you fail, you are encouraged, you encourage your partner, and you both work to find the teachings that will help both of you out of a similar situation in the future. When you develop a need or recognize something is missing in your life, your partner assists you in accomplishing and fulfilling your goals, and you do the same.

True partnership exists under these circumstances.

Sacrifice is not necessary.

Immaturity

Immaturity is a version of insecurity that affects all who are not secure in themselves. Not knowing the proper order of things or the procedure to approach an end effectively is never the problem. It is the inability or unwillingness to learn, adapt, grow, or transform into the ability not only to approach a desired end, but to coordinate and to cooperate with another that is the problem.

Partnership in its highest form pits two or more individuals together, working together to create a reality greater than the one they have created as a single individual. Two partners that are unequally yoked in a particular situation merely means that the roles are reversed. The highest qualities of an individual can be turned to a positive or a negative light. However, they are hardly good reasons for the relationship to fail. They are the more reasons for grand success.

Evaluate your insecurities. Focus on the positive aspects of your partner and notice the balance that may be trying to take place, but is being blocked by the insecurity lodged in your nature.

Irreconcilable Differences

The differences that separate partners are very rarely irreconcilable. Often they are differences in values and or beliefs, ideas about life that were given to the individual as a child. When these differences arise, the question is whether they will be enough to destroy the relationship. It is possible to adjust, change, or mesh the values and beliefs that two partners carry, propelling them to greater connection and partnership. The effort to do this however takes time because the ideas will be deeply ingrained.

What are your views on relationship, partnership? If this is an intimate relationship, what are your ideas on marriage, children, parenting, and money? What is required for each to feel safe, secure, and assured in the partnership? What are your views on food and health?

Take a look at each area of life. Evaluate each with deep questions, getting to the root of what is important and why. These will uncover deep differences that need to be addressed so that the partnership is not shaken at its core at an undisclosed point in the future.

The differences that arise in partnership are never a reason to create separation. They are excellent opportunity for greater understanding and deeper connection, but it requires strength on your part to open up to that possibility.

Financial Issues

Money is often a source of struggle for power in partnership. This is the result of one or two individuals who have never felt they had any control in their lives, and what greater way to finally be king or queen than to control the money in partnership.

A partnership and a team can have a close resemblance. In a true partnership there is balance, there is sharing, there is equal power. Just as in a team, each player carries equal levels of importance for the team to function properly and to be effective.

What are the financial goals of the partnership? What contribution is each partner able to make at the moment? Is the current plan fitting for everyone until future adjustments are necessary?

With a plan in place, move forward as a partnership. Move forward as a team.

The partnership that withstands the winds of struggle, whether they are financial or otherwise, gaining knowledge and understanding of the strengths, weaknesses, and the optimal positions for each player on the team, is much stronger in the end.

Insecurity

Insecurity is not a part of a partnership. It is brought into the partnership.

What past experiences, "in your life," have created skepticism in your mind as to the success of a partnership? Who was the culprit?

This is critical to know because whether or not you are still with that person physically, you are still with that person. Or, it may be events that you observed as a child that make you uneasy or anxious when it comes to relationships. Are you protecting yourself from getting hurt again, or, are you protecting yourself from getting hurt the way you have seen others being hurt?

If you bring these ideas into a relationship, into a new partnership, you are dooming it from the beginning. In your attempts to protect yourself, you are looking for the evidence of trouble and you will find it whether it is really there or not.

In addition to what you are looking for and what you see, the driving idea of the event that you are trying to avoid causes you to act in ways that are also in line with protecting yourself from hurt. You are not 100% compassionate, loving, caring, or understanding. You always have your guard up, and these behaviors are not in alignment with a successful partnership. They are in alignment with separation and broken relationships.

You must identify your insecurities, and quell the jealousy, shame, and guilt that may stem from them if you truly want success in partnership.

Barring the fact that your partner has given you reasons to be insecure, you brought insecurity to the party yourself.

Boredom/Complacency

Boredom and complacency are the result of a lack of effort to create excitement and spontaneity.

Is anyone at fault, or has life taken precedence over the health of the partnership? Well, placing fault or blame is the wrong approach altogether.

If the partnership is true, then a discussion to rekindle the fire of life in the partnership should be fun and eye opening. It is possible that interests have changed, likes have changed, and the priority list of desires and things to experience have changed as well. So the list of options and opportunities should be worthwhile.

Take responsibility for creating new fun and excitement in the partnership. Collaborate with your partner to create opportunities for connection, closeness, and life.

Distance

Distance does require a little extra effort when it comes to a relationship, and it matters at what stage in the relationship the required distance between partners becomes a factor.

Presence is created in the mind of the partner you are with through your words and the sharing of experiences, and these are able to be created through technology, but the physical, energetic presence of a partner is also desirable.

The stage at which the distance becomes a factor is critical because of the understanding and trust that may or may not have developed. Trust is critical in a partnership, for the weight of constant worry and wonder as to the whereabouts and doings of a partner is detrimental. It destroys the relationship because your role is tainted by thoughts and feelings that are not in alignment with growth, development, and closeness.

Distance does not have to be a negative factor as long as you are aware that the areas such as closeness, connection, and trust must be developed through other means because of the distance.

The Real Self Emerges

The true self of any one individual is only ever revealed over time. This is the misunderstood fact of partnerships and relationships. The true person behind the smiles and presentation of a person's best self emerges when the inevitable conflict between two individuals begins to mount...

This is also the area that you want to give much consideration and effort because it is the unknown variable. Until you and your partner are in certain situations, you do not know how they are going to respond. You do not know who they are in those instances; when faced with exceptional experiences.

What are their driving ideas about life? How do they handle failure and loss? What did they learn and believe as true in the areas of relationships, marriage, parenting, family?

Who will they be when the newness of the partnership wears off?

The true self of a partner can be scary. It can be frustrating. It can be an entirely different person.

Take time to get to know your partner. Explore all areas of life and find out their ideas. Find out their past life experiences and how they do or may impact their present with you.

Dishonesty/Deception

Dishonesty and deception are the perfect way to start a relationship with holes and cracks in the foundation.

Whether you are trying to protect your ego, or the mind and heart of your partner, dishonesty and deceit create separation between you and your partner that, once discovered, may be irreversible.

In relationship trust is paramount. If you cannot trust your partner with all of your fears, with all of your desires, with all of your deepest secrets, there will always be a divide between you and the person you hold most dear.

Truth is the play of power in a partnership. Honesty is admirable even when it does not feel so good.

When your partner knows all of the pieces of you, and they choose to support you anyway, now you have something.

Criticism

Being observant to changes that need to be made, or constantly looking for ways to improve is one thing, but being overly critical is something else.

Criticism takes on a damaging nature when it is constantly directed at an individual. Most strong, confident individuals gladly accept ideas different from their own, and want to improve, but, constant complaints, disappointments and unhappiness about your partner tears at the fabric of closeness and connection.

Often when you look closely at a person who tends to be critical of others, you find that the individual is highly critical of himself or herself. Therefore, that is the person they tend to be with those closest to them. Partners, spouses, and children are all fair game to these individuals, and this behavior does not build relationships. It tears them down.

Check to see that your focus is not on the problems at present, but on the formulation, and execution of solutions. Assistance and help are grand when they are asked for. When they are not solicited, they often fall on deaf ears and on an upset, frustrated conscious.

Leave your critical nature at the door. Be the person who builds up instead of being the person who tears down, and watch the results in your relationship.

Fairy Tale Fantasies

Yes, it is unrealistic to believe that every moment of everyday will be beautiful and sweet in the sense that there will never be conflict and that there will never be opportunities to learn and discuss differences of opinion.

Life is about growth and expansion, and the individuals that commit to being in relationship with you are your greatest teachers, for they assist you in uncovering those areas in your life where you need to release and let go of ideas that may separate you from other people. They also make you aware of knew ideas that draw, connect, and enhance your partnership.

Expect that there will be opportunities to grow. Expect that there will be differences of opinion and understanding. This is what makes relationships rich with possibilities.

The question is, are you open to the possibilities. Are you open to acquiring the skills that place you in the forefront as a creator of a relationship?

These are the questions.

You Think Your Happiness is Dependent On Someone Else

Your happiness is yours, and completion leads to pain.

Partnership is not a situation where another person fills the voids of your soul. Whatever you feel like you are missing or did not get as a child is not for your partner to fill. This is a huge unconscious mistake when it comes to relationship. For a brief moment you may be fulfilled, and for that reason you feel loved and cared for because you are getting something, mentally and/or emotionally, that has been absent previously. The challenge is that if your partner ever stops, or something happens so that they can no longer deliver, now the void is no longer being filled and you quickly fall out of what you call and believe to be love.

The fragments of your heart and soul need putting together. They are not meant to be patched by any individual outside of you, and bringing these fragments into a relationship only creates pressure on the whole. You must make a practice of uncovering the fragments of your heart. You must also recognize that if you have ever been happy before, you can take it with you.

You can generate the fragments right now, and put them back together. You can generate the happiness right now, and take it with you wherever you go.

This is the difference from feeling the heat, and being the fire.

You Allow Others To Treat You With Disrespect

In relationship, people treat you in direct accordance with the way you subconsciously think and feel about yourself.

If you have low self-worth, if you believe yourself to be lucky to have a partner or to be in a relationship, if you do not see yourself as valuable in the equation of the partnership you will be treated in that light.

Inner strength and a presence that commands respect sets the tone for the partnership. We are not talking about a dominating nature and associated behaviors. We are talking about an inner knowing that relationship is a complementing association, and that the value, the person that you bring into the cooperation is just as important as anyone else.

Look to your value and your worth. Notice its presence or lack of presence in all situations, and seek to build it by observing your value, your input, the wisdom, knowledge, and experience you bring to the table.

Learning to value and cherish yourself is the first and most important step to teaching others to value and cherish you.

Poor Communication

Lack of communication tends to be the coup de grace of disaster in many relationships, and encompasses many of the reasons we have discussed. Poor communication breeds a lack of trust, insecurity, fear, worry and doubt about the relationship.

Poor communication can be caused by preexisting insecurities or a quest to keep certain areas of life private so as not to lose individuality. These lead to the decline and death of the relationship. Each leads to related negative effects that slowly become factors, points of concern and conflict in the partnership.

Communication between partners should be spontaneous and scripted, to ensure that all topics are discussed. Communication should be respectful, but open and honest. If you never say how you truly feel or express your desires, you cannot expect your partner to assist, support, or attempt to deliver on them.

True communication sets the tone for embarking on the greatest of undertakings, which is relationship. Relationship is an undertaking, which, at its core, uncovers all personality and character deficiencies and weaknesses that separate you from successful partnership, thus giving you the opportunity to correct them, or continue to experience broken forms of a relationship repeatedly.

All that can and is revealed starts with the level and nature of communication you choose to utilize in partnership.

Conclusion

The top reasons why relationships fail is an eye opening summary of those critical, often unseen areas and factors that bring relationships crumbling to the ground. As you look back on each topic, you will notice that each requires a bit of self-discovery, a look inward to the causes of conflict and challenge in the relationships in your personal experience.

The partnerships discussed in these chapters not only pertain to intimate relationships but work associations as well.

I congratulate you on becoming a part of the family, and taking steps on the journey to becoming Brilliant in every area of your life.

LOVE

In Spirit I Thrive, In Mind I Fall. It Is My Job, To Unify Them All.

I now realize that for two decades I have been striving to release the true, authentic me that had been covered by fear-based ideas and perceptions. (Get Past Yourself)

I am realizing that the life I once lived, and the life story that is being lived around me by family and friends is not a chosen life, but one that has been passed along. With elements of fear at its base, loss, pain, failure, and the embarrassment of mistake once defined me, now they propel me. (The Other Side Of Fear)

Now I strive to allow the true, authentic, Source inspired me to breathe through at every moment. This grants me the knowing that my desires are pure and in line with the path that is specifically for me. (Allowing Me)

I did not need a teacher, a preacher, or a guru. All I needed was some Guidance and some Direction. (My Only Need)

Benny

The Rest Of The Series

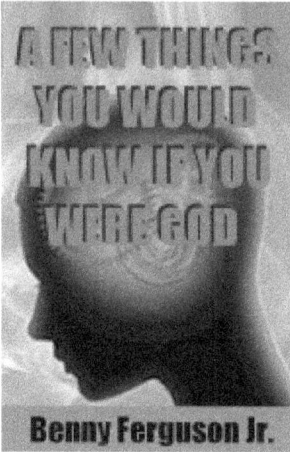

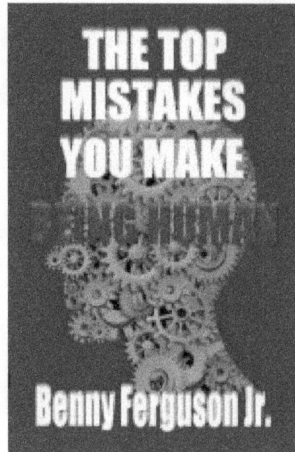

Connecting With Benny:

Facebook: www.facebook.com/bennyrfergusonjr

Youtube: www.youtube.com/BennyFergusonJr/videos

Twitter: www.twitter.com/BennyRFergusonJ

Contacting Benny:

Initial contacts to Benny for discussions, interviews, one – on - one or group coaching, speaking or training may be made through telephone or email.

Phone: 336-546-7142

Email: BennyFerguson@TheFergusonCompany.com